The Man Molded From Mud

VACENTA RAKEY

The Man Molded From Mud

Copyright © 2022 by Vacenta Rakey

Published by Lightning Fast Book Publishing, LLC

www.lfbookpublishing.com

The author of this book offers inspirational and reflective poetry concerning his journey and evolution as a man. In the event that you use or enact any of the material in this book, the author and publisher assume no responsibility for your actions.

ISBN: 979-8-9852917-4-2

Table of Contents

FEEL THE LOVE

THE COST OF FREE

ACTIVATE YOURSELF

Preface

Every poem in this book is special and has its own identity. Each one was written from a place of confinement yet a place of love. On the day I read a poem written by Tupac "The Rose that Grew from Concrete," I was inspired to pick up a pen and write my first poem.

"The Man Molded From Mud," is anyone who is facing or has faced adversity and overcame it with gratitude, which is also the definition of my brand Kalfmuscle Gang. Many times in life, we focus on the problem instead of the solution and end goal From this day forward, let's hold peace in our mind and love in our hearts, which will help us endure the trials and obstacles of the world.

Dedication

I would like to give a special thanks to God for the strength and mind power to complete this project. This book is dedicated to Grams(RIH) Audi, Milli, K Roc, Nephew, Crusha, Flare, Kandi, Trea, Grandda, Aunt Neat(RIH), Mac, Kollins, Mya, Britney, Juice, Knotrah, Sherilynne, Bridget, Angie, Aunt Sib, Pops, Chelly, Mr. Bobby, Mrs. Gill and E, all who held me down and/or motivated me to keep pushing and pursuing. I would also like to give a special shout out to Cuzoo!, Byrd, Savage, Vito, C Notes, Destiny, Pulley, Ben, Tilly, Trap Money, Phil, Neff, 99Twon, Tim, Latimoe, Curt, Mrs. Sophy, Ms. Van, Stacy, Mr. Ben, Mrs. Lynn, Hoodrich Keem, Lasha(RIH), Uncle Garfield, Shavon, Rizzy, MB, Shane Dane and all of my god-kids, ALL of You. I appreciate everyone of you all from the bottom of my heart.

WAKE UP

"PotS ReveN"

8-29-19

Giving up should be no option, and

Quitting cannot be selected

Any thoughts of the two

Should be quickly neglected

Let it marinate in your mind

That your dreams come first

And when doubt comes about

Read this title "Reversed"

-Dedicated to Kaden

"Follow the Voice
of the Righteous"
1-14-20

Heard from such a distance

is a voice telling me what's healthy

specifies are very articulate

but my heart is still selfish

Confusion controls my environment

Of my ways, I'm feeling retirement

Maybe it's the voice,

or maybe this aptness is becoming tiring

I know I know what's right,

am I wrong if I contradict?

This crossroad appears often

finding it difficult to depict.

Following the voice in the dark

I stumble and sometimes fall

but no matter what happens along the way

I get up and give it my all

Maybe the voice is my God,
Maybe the voice is myself
Either way, the farther it is away
the more it seems to help

Expecting instant gratification
could be the reason I choose my choice
but I think it's time I evolve
and follow the encouraging voice

"Peripateo"
1-15-20

Life is a gift, freedom is a privilege

Living is a choice, we're all born in prison

To try it on your own is a choice that is given

But the best way, is to be led by the spirit

Traveling this journey, we must all walk by faith

Earth is temporary with demands to be great

What we must do, is control our pace,

and know through earthly behaviors our future is
shaped

To "walk around" the world may take forever or a day,

depending on how you travel and the route you take

Walk by faith, and not by sight

because the way you walk will shape your life

"Patience Is…"

11-8-19

Patience is a key which can unlock many doors

Patience is a weapon that can win many wars

Patience is much needed with the world moving fast

Patience is priority if you wish to surpass

Patience is medicine, it'll soon heal wounds

Patience is the bridge that makes forever feel soon

Patience is like water, you must have it in order to live

Patience is the tunnel through everything is revealed

Patience is a mirror with a double sided affect

Patience is self control, which is what patience reflects

Patience is strength along with power and courage

Patience, if infant must be fostered and nourished

Patience is a virtue which shows character and quality

So, always show patience and sit aside velocity

"Fortune Favors the Brave"

11-24-19

For every risk, there lies a reward
    do not be afraid to try and go for it
Stepping stones are fine
    but don't let working control your days
Take a shot at your dreams, and remember
    fortune favors the brave

"Difficult Waters"
12-11-19

At the beginning things were

shallow understanding and clear

as things get deeper

came panic and fear

it's hard to stay afloat

because waves are way too violent

this is a wave of life,

one you can't just stop, riding

winds erupt with rage

as if life is now being punished

the water never lies

even with pollution it remains honest

the farther you go out

thoughts of failure are aborted

with chances to live or die

which to you is most important

"Strength of an African"

12-15-19

Grass, it sprouts from the earth

through concrete or through dirt

It's hard to block it from growing

like stopping a star from glowing

Roots are strong, piercing through rock and brick

they even grow long enough to climb a fence

Grass doesn't need to be planted

to grow under any circumstances;

The brightness of the green signifies

earth as one, being identified

as the peaceful united force

that helps ground remain on course

Grass represents beauty and strength,

adding light to the dark and healing to the sick

once it is accepted

It should then be respected

as an important product of life

and as courage whenever in sight

"Survival Kit"

12-15-19

What's up son, can you please do me a favor?

Remain strong and seek wisdom

While staying free from all haters,

life may get hard

still don't expect nothing to be given

Overcoming hardships

is what makes life worth living

constructive criticism will be given only to help

Don't let it get you emotional

Keep control over yourself

Accept discipline as your friend

There's no need to follow the crowd

Read this message until it's recollected,

though it may take a while

Always show kindness

but don't expect it in return

Give respect as it is given

because respect is something you earn

Don't look to man for answers
instead place your faith in God
and no matter what happens in life, I promise
you'll always beat the odds

-For Kaden
-For All my seeds
-For The Youth

"Lifted From Under The Rock"

12-18-19

For a long period of time

I was stuck under a rock

To be free was a feeling

completely surrounded by doubt

But honesty lifted me up

and courage held my hand

Valiance guided my path

when integrity gave me a chance

So, today I am free

and no longer live under a rock

Keys have been found

and doors are unlocked

"Don't think About it Too Much"

12-18-19

Think for a second, but not a second too long
If it's real, may it remain,
    If it's false, may it be gone
Think for a minute, but not a minute too long
Delete it if it's weak,
    keep it, if it's strong
Think for an hour, but not an hour too long,
because out in the world,
    is where thoughts belong
Think for a day, but not a day too long
not all thoughts should be entertained,
    some are best left alone

"A Simple Alternative"
12-19-19

Changing the way you think
can change the way you live
Many times it's something small
It's not always something big

"The Gift of Life"
12-25-19

The Gift of Life can be described as,
sharing, giving, caring, and feelings,
which can all be taken for granted
Share experiences, give lots of hugs,
care for one another, and feel the love

The Gift of Life can be described as
skies, land, sun, and rain,
which can all be taken for granted
Give thanks to the skies, appreciate the land
Absorb sunlight, and give rain a chance

The Gift of Life can come in many ways
such as a child, a parent, an enemy or a friend
So, cherish the Gifts of Life,
before this, as we know life ends

"Comes and Gos of Troubles"
12-26-19

When smiles turn to frowns

and laughs turn to cries

the sun will go down

tears will fall from the skies

hold on to what you know

and release knowledge you have,

which is, trouble always come

but trouble don't always last

tears will be dried

from the face and the skies

pain will soon cease,

and joy will then rise

when your days take a turn

be prepared to stay humble

overall things are great

through the comes and gos of troubles

"Defeat vs. Success"
11-7-19

Sometimes I feel defeated,

and at times, I feel attainment

The times I feel conquered

I'm reminded it's no one I'm racing

The feeling of failure lies within

I know I fail if I fail to begin

What about in the eyes of my people

if I fail will they feel that we all are equal

Success embarks in your mind

First, you must think it in order to be

Make sure your plan is divine

with ambition to achieve it to any degree

"Cast Your Desires"

11-10-19

Be precise about your wishes,

then cast them into the world

without exception of any details

prepare yourself to prevail

Being specific about your dreams

will cause accurate results

faith combined with effort

along with commitment will make it better

God will present your desires

as long as you let him know what you wish

the power of thought is important

whatever you think is what you'll get

"L.I.V.E."

11-12-19

Have you ever been ready
ready to leave, love or live
or just ready to experience
what life really is?

Have you ever been ready
to Increase, Impress, and improve
while experiencing life
at a higher altitude?

Have you ever been ready
for volition, to value, and vision
and approach life
with more precise decisions?

Have you ever been ready
to elevate, excel, and explore?
If so open your mind
and be receptive to more.

"Wondrous Diversions"
11-20-19

With plans to go right, I somehow turned left

Though I've gotten off course, I happened to learn self

Blessings within the lessons was enough to open my eyes,

and I now look at this time as a sign sent from God

I'm no longer anxious but I feel I'm prepared

to move from this stage with a mind that is repaired

So, I give it my all and let God do the rest

while the road I chose turned out to be the best

"Look Towards the Stars"

11-21-19

For your questions and inquiries

Hold them till the night fall

It's hard to control them all

Look towards the stars

to find out who you are

When you receive your answers

and confirmation for things you asked,

give thanks to the stars

for replacing the solutions you lack

Look towards the stars

to remove all your scars

When looking back on your past,

thinking how you made it and why,

Do not be ashamed with your head held high

to look up and give thanks to the sky

Look towards the stars

"Levels of Levels"
11-23-19

It's a level above the level you're on

and a level above where you're trying to go

There's a level above the one you were on

from where you are is a level below

The level you're on will prepare your mind

for the level to come, so you won't rewind

The next level in life will take courage and valor,

which is what helped you succeed from the level before

Two levels ago you felt pity and ruth,

which makes the level you're on feel failure-proof

But take no level for granted and always stay humble

No matter the level you're on, they all come with troubles

Prepare yourself for the next level,

which is growth and success

and once you get there, start to prepare yourself

for the next

"Take Time
Without Wasting Time"

11-24-19

It's a thin line between

taking time and wasting time,

so be careful how you use it

Don't waste ya mind

Don't waste ya grind

on nothing that is not beneficial

because time is important

and if wasted can be an issue

Learn to use what you have

and don't stress what you need

because time used right

is all it takes to achieve

Take ya time without wasting time

but remember it's a thin line

Don't focus on a finish line

just know that all time is winning time

"Food for Thought"
11-29-19

Feed your muscles, your mental, and your spirit
pay attention, if you feel it, you should listen
wrapped up in fast paced life gets hectic
slow down, cause in the midst, there's a message

Feed your spirit, your mental, and your muscles
muscles are strength, combined with mental they double
spirit is discernment which will order all your steps
so, with all three combined, this defines all your help

"Readers' Title_____________"

11-29-19

As I look around, I take in what I notice

I gratify what I feel, I accept who I am

still I reach for change

but it's just beyond my grasp

maybe I should reach a little further

to get what I deserve

because change is a cure

but acceptance comes first

"Knowledge"
7-4-19

It comes in two forms, general and specialized

Specialized is the one we often fail to recognize

Many men seek it and on a daily basis they chase it

But once they possess it, they do nothin; equivalent to passion

Stop for a second and think, do you know what you know

Or is it all assumed to be thought, you learn as you go

Cause some don't go far, and some don't go at all

It seems though the farther you go, the more they say you know it all

But continue to think, those thoughts soon become actions

Those actions become history and that history becomes magic

What is magic? A fraction of the potential prudence you contracted

So always seek it, and never get complacent

And if you ask; ask for nothing less than inspiration

It's enlightenment, cognition and science as well

So use your "knowledge" wisely, and wisdom will soon prevail

"Decoded Perfection"
11-30-19

Speak in a language so your people understand

and let them be influenced as you do the best you can

Speak motivation but show inspiration

Nothing that you do will fall under basic

Became the greatest over time

as you perfect your craft

Now millions will be inspired to walk in your path

Speak motivation but show inspiration

and the world will be changed by your act of dedication

-To Antonio Evans

"Step by Step"
11-30-19

Follow before you lead, and once you lead continue to learn
Knowledge must be attained to gain anything more you earn
Next comes wisdom, and wisdom is the key
to unlock locked doors and set your mind free

FEEL THE LOVE

"There's a Melody Within"

1-12-20

Grateful for every blessing

She would sing for refreshment

acceptance of life's lessons

She would sing instead of stressing

extending assistance to all

She would sing a song so warm

such a melody so sweet within,

She would dance and praise the Lord

leading the blind from darkness

She would dance when they come aboard

nurturing the avid and hungry

She would dance when everyone came

even alone with love in her heart

She would dance and praise His name

such a melody so sweet within,

Her praising would make you smile

through good times and bad times

She would dance and sing aloud

-For Alberta E. Foggie (RIH Grams)

"Love"
8-3-19

Let it spread throughout

Seek it if you doubt

It's not easily captured

But it's easily mastered

To a chosen few, it comes natural

If showing a lot to the righteous

But showing more to the bastard

A room once filled with disasters

Is now a room filled with laughter

If you ever felt the feeling

and didn't know what it was

You now know the most powerful

feeling is love

"Love Live Energy"
9-20-19

The energy transferred from one soul to the next
can have a negative effect or a positive reject
be cautious of the energy you accept as well as select
and have discernment to a level you can easily detect
bad vibes and good vibes and energy that is pure
if bad energy becomes contagious use sympathy as a cure
use positive energy to live and let the frequency live on
so, even when you expire, your energy is still strong

"1215225 Interstate"

9-5-19

Have patience with my heart

It'll soon reveal my love

Get acquainted with my touch

So it's familiar when we hug

Put your trust in my thoughts

And I'll never lead you wrong

Join me on this road

So, neither of us is alone

Though this road may be long

We'll walk this journey together

And since you had patience with my heart

You now have my love forever

"A Reason to Love"
9-8-19

Let's toast to this special moment

Normally I wouldn't condone it

But yesterday I was lonely

Now a feeling has come on me and I cherish it strongly

Forever it stands; it won't break but may bend

The roots run deep, so no fears of the wind

We can now ignore the threats that come from the storm

because today on this earth a reason to love was born

"From Love Until"

10-9-19

Tenuous is overcome by force

Affliction is overcome by felicity

Death is overcome by Life

And Love —goes to infinity

"Parental Love"

10-10-19

The love from a mother to a son

is unequivocal

The love from a father to a daughter

is exceptional

Parental love is the same as

Medicine for a child

It can create guidance stability

and help them reconcile

Show your children love

and let them know they have a purpose

because they are the future,

it is for them we are working

"Escape the Pain Through My Love"

10-15-19

Follow the path of my love

with your heart, and not your feet

As I lead you away from pain

our hearts will start to sync

Distress from your past is expressed on your face

but follow the path of my love, and soon it'll all erase

The closer you get, the more it will hurt

because before it gets better, it will always get worse

Once you escape the pain, you'll find yourself at a gate

The other side holds my love, a place you'll always be safe

"Aborting Love"

12-19-19

If my love starts to bore you

please let me know,

so we can find a solution

Before stupor starts to grow,

communicate with me please

instead of breaking my heart

Though it will hurt if you leave

dishonesty will tear it apart

I'm willing to let you go

if separation will make you happy

but first let me know,

what is it, my love, what happened?

"Don't Forget Love"
12-18-19

Speak Love

Show Love

Give Love

Eat Love

Sleep Love

Be Love

Just Love

"Love Bound"

1-3-20

Place your heart in my hands,

so I can put my love in it

If you're nervous, let me know

so i'm aware of how to send it

if you're confident it will show,

leaving your previous love suspended

if you're willing to let it flow

love will run its course till we're winded

with your heart in my hands

and my love in your heart

against the world we will stand

united as one, and not apart

"Love Junction"
1-23-19

As things come together,

our love will be forever

grateful for your teachings

and I'm thankful for your speeches

enlightening with your aura

with an attitude uplifting

a lot to offer earth

for together we're existing

positive vibes and genuine manners

this is history in the making;

the power of calmness is felt

through a very remarkable sensation

hold on to my radiance

so if ever you feel out of tune

the connection of our spirits

will shine with love as bright as the moon

To be where two hearts meet

-With thoughts of TR

"Hear My Heart"

7-27-19

My heart is full of passion

But don't take my love for granted

Although It's slowly healing

You can still see the damage

Caused by someone

I adored very dearly

Open your ears as I speak from my heart

Now tell me can you hear me

My love is roaring loud

As I speak through my heart

Though it's still filled with passion

It's starting to feel dark

"Cupid's Marathon"

12-11-19

We were both shot in the back

by cupid's sharp arrow

the road once wide

is now illiberal and narrow

through the arrows in our back

the love drug was injected

our minds became familiar

and our hearts became connected

what time does to love

it sometimes leaves it with no choice,

but to respect the fact

that love just sometimes runs its course

"Can You Still Love Me?"
8-30-19

Could you still love me, or maybe I should ask

would you still love me

If my possessions were low

And the only thing I owned

Was my love to show,

No cars, no house, just roaming through the world

Could my love alone be enough

To win you as my girl

What if my shoes was not acceptable

And neither was my clothes

But through all of my imperfections

My love still showed

I hope you can still love me

Because your love maybe all I need

To become all that I am

And begin to proceed

"Love the Future"
9-2-19

The love directed towards a child
Is filled with value, passion, and patience
It's the type of love
That can never suffer replacement

The love that surrounds a child
Can be tough, tender, merciful, yet firm
It's the type of love
That is unconditional, and not learned

The love that is instilled in a child
Will reflect in their actions
So always shower your child
With high quality love and passion

"My lovely One"
10-13-19

No words can express

the way I truly feel

Many times I fantasize

and the visions seem real

My heart has never experienced

the mirth I get from you

As if God read my mind

and made my wishes come true

I'd give it all up to touch you, kiss you

or only to see your face

My stomach gets filled with butterflies

and my heart increases in pace

fancy cars money and houses

but still it's not the same to me

I prayed and waited and wished on a star

and finally you came to me

"The Heartache
I Suffer"

11-16-19

The heartache I suffer

because of the love I thought was there

It is all my fault being the fact

how could I expect them to care

about decisions I made that led to darkness

and choices I made that weren't the smartest

expecting a letter or a card to express

their love for me instead of feeling neglect

The heartache I suffer is now turning me dull

so soon as I'm home I'll return the love

"The Moment Love Was Found"

12-2-19

The minute was right

the hour was cool

the second was perfect

the beauty was you

What I found was great

a blessing from above

what I experienced was real

what I felt was love

Where I arrived was bliss

Where I left was pain

sorrow was lost

while love was gained

"Love Me First"

1-30-20

Feel how you feel but if it's real
>love me first
lies will be revealed as pain starts to heal, still,
>love me first
knowing it truly hurts and I deserve worse, please;
>love me first
To a gift from a curse it's funny how it works, still;
>love me first
neglect your mind accompanying your heart this time, please;
>love me first
Our bond resembles a vine adopting the concept of wine, still;
>love me first
If this doesn't work my heart will need a nurse, please;
>love me first
No more tears let go of your fears, please;
>love me first
I love you first I love you after, so will you now
>love me first
Through actions your heart is captured, and this is how
>Our love will work

"Mama's Love"
1-16-19

Whenever I couldn't breathe
Mama's love presented air
at times I felt lonely
Mama's love was always there
reducing most of the pain
Mama's love is like a remedy
When nobody was around
Mama's love was a friend to me
Never say never, but
Mama's love never ceased
Whenever I couldn't sleep, I put
Mama's love on repeat
at times I am cold
Mama's love is my sweater
And when I was locked up
Mama's love came in a letter
I thank you, Mama
For an unconditional love
There's no Mama like you Mama
Truly sent from above

-Dedicated to Milli

"Love Doesn't Discriminate"
1-1-20

The time span has been short

but this feeling is so strong

love doesn't judge,

so how could this be wrong

I feel we've known each other for long

no doubt we were meant to be

we can't ignore this passion,

or avoid this chemistry

you know just where it hurts

I know what brings you joy

love doesn't discriminate,

it's the feeling we employ

where no time can be placed

it's all based on vibes

time can't infer

when two heart will collide

"The Love Below"
10-5-19

Deep down below in the depths
lies broken pieces of a heart
They're slowly healing themselves
enduring the coldness and the dark
Injured, stomped on, and even stabbed from behind
the heart is rising from below, searching hard to find
Love, affection, and another heart to match
as time goes by, it's amending from the past
With damages slowly vanishing
It's becoming stronger than ever before
With love assigned to managing
the heart is surfacing up from the floor
now that it's able to breath
and the pieces are all together
The love below is at ease
and the heart can now soar forever

"Love's Bad Side"

10-31-19

Love can be scary,
especially going into it blind
Love can be temporary
it's very dependent on time

Love can be a fright
and suddenly darken the light in your life
Love can become a plight
the type that is difficult to get back right

Love can be a nightmare
one that's reality and not just a dream
so with love all in the air
be cautious of how you breath

Though love can be terror
intimidating and horror
love can also ascend you to ecstasies
you've never experienced before

"Revenge From a Broken Heart"

1-9-19

I couldn't care any less

about your broken heart or hurt feelings

Where was you heart

when I was in need of attention?

Slowly gaining my senses

and my heart is proudly cold

No longer ashamed to mention

the grudged I'm ready to hold

For your heart to crumble in pieces

is something I often yearn

Repeatedly I've been hurt,

Congratulations, It's your turn

Follow behind me closely

as we enter the gates of misery

and be prepared to welcome

pain, agony, and karma,literally.

THE COST OF FREE

"Beautiful Fruit"

12-30-19

What is planted shall grow

From the mind to the earth

What is granted shall flow

Which is a sign from birth

While thoughts are presented

Actions become relentless

Access to your intellect

Become tanglible and endless

Character results from thinking

Which makes it hard to hide notion

All thoughts are shared

Rather through words or through motion

So let your mind stay pure

And your intentions be true

For life, you will be sure

To bear beautiful fruit

"Sanity"

12-29-19

Peace is as sound

As sound is peace

With peace all around

We will all get relief

Introducing peace

To a world full of violence

Is the same as bringing music

To a room full of silence

Sound is as peace

As peace is sound

Wherever there is grief

May sound and peace be found

"The Beauty Beyond"

12-7-19

The beauty of the grass
Matches the beauty of the skies
The creation was a task
Completed all by God

Man was created
To add substance to the earth
I'm sure earth would agree
Since we've arrived it's been worse

The beauty of life
Matches the beauty of living
With no right or wrong
Our purpose is giving

The beauty of the mind
Matches the beauty of the land
Because what God didn't create
Was created by man

"When The Sun Cried"

12-16-19

In the middle of the night

As the sun shines bright

The moon shines brighter

And the clouds are much lighter

Inside of this stigma

Is a long lost dilemma

That was chosen out of anger

Now the sun is in danger

As it gleams throughout the night

Some feel it isn't right

And shouldn't shine till the morning

Giving darkness no warning

By waiting till tomorrow

This created pain and sorrow

Only wanting to shine

Pushing its pride to the side

There's grieving in the skies

On the day the sun cried

"The Gift of Life"

12-25-19

The gift of life can be described as
Sharing, giving, caring and feelings
Which can all be taken for granted
Share experiences give lots of hugs
Care for one another and feel the love

The gift of life can be described as
Skies, land, sun and rain
Which can all be taken for granted
Give thanks to the skies, appreciate the land
Absorb sunlight and give the rain a chance

The gift of life can come in many ways
Such as a child, a parent, an enemy or friend
So cherish the gifts of life
Before this as we know life ends

"Roots of Discernment"

1-6-20

Things get deeper the further you go

To explain in a time frame

With understanding

May make it seem more so shallow

To understand life may take a lifetime

The average man can't comprehend

And goes through life

Without ever developing his right mind

Understanding is a big enemy of impatience

An unseen force can throw us off course

Or be an asset

It's materials that make man complacent

Manage your time, as land is conquered

Walk by faith and be led by grace

Understanding comes in many forms

But once it's gained and maintained it's followed by honor

"A Letter to Time"
11-17-19

Thank you for having patience with me
And understanding my judgment, I know i've
Made you angry but you never held any grudges, I
Appreciate your teachings as well as the lessons, this
Is a thank you note as well as a confession, in the
Past i've insulted you and taken you for granted, so
This is my restitution for suffering and damages, when I
Was stagnant it was you who stood by my side, but when
I started back moving still I overlooked you with pride,
When I was moving fast the only thing I was racing
To see was that no matter what I was doing, time was
Having patience with me.
Thank you time.

Vacenta

"Blessings That Flow From the River"

1-3-20

As I walk along the river

Watching as the moon reflects itself

The night is calm as ever

Peace is right and bedlam is left

The sound of nature at night

And the sight is refined still waters

Is a soul soothing scenery

Creating harmony followed by order

The river flows endless

As long as I walk, blessings will flow

But night doesn't last forever

At sunrise, I must go

The benefits will last forever

As long as the river and I are connected

In truth I believe this to be

The best way to receive my blessing

Forever I am grateful for a place to console me

Hold me and clean me with waters that are holy

"Let's Explore"
11-16-19

As I take off and leave earth

It's you who will be by my side

I'm only taking my mind

Leaving behind my ego and pride

Ride with me baby let's rise

Accompanied by stars and skies

Holding on to whatever we find

So if there's a storm we will be fine

The rain will symbol our cries

The sun will heal us as it shines

We left earth to escape all the lies

But we must return in order to refine

"Through Rain and Pain"

11-15-19

My life has been lived through rain and pain

For without you here joy isn't the same

From the moment we met I knew I was blessed

The rain then ceased and the pain was less

Through rain and pain I'm no longer shame

Only smiles and bliss since the day you came

Please remain close, your presence is my cure

As long as we're together, we will easily endure

I hand over the keys for now you are in charged

So please take care, with high regards

I don't regret the storm and hurt and it's you whom I blame

Cause in the midst of the rain and during the pain, you

Somehow magically came

"Eccentric Emotions"
11-22-19

Feelings and dreams along with material things

Often offer a hinder

Emotions can bring an abundance of things

And leave us with much to remember

Petitions and desires can initiate fires

Which are sometimes hard to put out

Affections are higher with sparks from the fire

Which eliminates feelings of doubt

Passion is low like the love below

Starting to birth feelings of sadness

If it gains control the rest will show

That whatever is destined will happen

Feelings, they change, and dreams, they change

They seldom remain the same

Wishes bring stains and love is pain

Emotions are more often strange

"The Rusty Metal"

7-28-19

Rusty metal is rough, rigid and

Less appealing to the eye

Through it's loud when you rub it

Deep down inside it is shy

With chips of paint here and there

People pass and don't glare

Hearing the rusty metal cry

But no one cares to even care

Brown and discolored

But distinctive as well

Unique beyond the eye

Something very few could tell

Maybe a sand down or a touch up with the brush

With only one thing missing it's still missing much

Perhaps some special attention

But no one seems to bother

And stop to realize

The Rusty Metal is the child with no father.

"Medicine of The Music"

12-14-19

The sounds of the music

Add solace to my heart

Vibrations are heartfelt

By the science and the art

Music is my medicine

When the world distributes burdens

Rescuing me from pain

The music is care and urgent

Nice fine tunes

From pianos, guitars, and drums

Give peace to my heart

And bring air to my lungs

Not only will I always accept

The medicine of the music

But as long as I live

I will always use it

"Her Poison"

11-23-19

Her eyes are soothing but her looks can kill

Her smile is proving that magic is real

Her body is doing something I feel

It's us in a union with all revealed

Lust is now cruising like an automobile

And I am now viewing; she is of steel

Her mind is renewing; she's accepting this thrill

Her tone is seducing and luring me near

What am I doing? I've never been here

What am I viewing? My visions not clear

Her body's not moving although it appears

Her lips are moving and i'm all ears

Hope this doesn't ruin what took years to build

But she is a beauty, and that's what I fear

"Peace Found In Solitude"

12-7-19

Alone here I sit as I reflect back on time

My heart well at ease and peace within my mind

In the depths of solitude is where I find myself

I say It many times because everyone else has left

Moments spent alone filled with time, wisdom and love

I don't mind sharing neither but there never is enough

My time is taken for granted and my wisdom goes unnoticed

No way my love is a factor cause my heart had long been broken

But isolation understands and this is enough for me

Because peace within solitude is enough to set you free

"Adopting & Aborting"

12-24-19

Insecurities now living once laid dormant

Yesterday they were powerless; today they bring torment

Giving power over your body; they've taken over your mind

Decisions now made with them as a cosign

Easy come easy go but how did insecurities grow

Never mind that, it's time for confidence to show

With your head held high it's time to reclaim

Confidence you once had through a very powerful change

"Consciousness"
7-16-19

Let consciousness do the work
Don't interfere with the flow
Learn to response from your soul
Instead of your ego
Realize that nothing is personal
The universe acts through you
So whatever you put into the atmosphere
Is what life is going to give back to you
Look out for change and use it wisely
But wait until your intentions are clear
Remember, God is in control
But you must help him steer
Accept the experience that's in front of you
Remain calm in the presence of stress
Keep faith in all you imagine
And the world will do the rest

"Expensive Emotions"
7-18-19

The voice in my heart tells me to love and forgive
But the voice in my head says that love isn't real
My heart is caring, kind, tender but yet brave
The thoughts in mind are results of things
I crave
The voice in my heart reminds me that loving is free
Then the voice in my head reminds me that nothing
Is free
If you want love, you must invest time or love in return
There will always be a price to pay for
The emotions we earn
Rather it be sadness or joy, madness or excitement
The voice in my head reminds me no emotions
Are priceless

"In The Midst
of Ecstasy"

8-14-19

In the midst of ecstasy, 2 structures exist

With two things in common, passion and a wish

With no need to speak

Emotions are extremely loud

The body takes over

Mute to all sounds

This is the moment I look in your eyes

Before our next stage arise

You lay in my arms as the moon dissolves

I kiss your soft lips as the sunshine calls

I enjoyed your company but now I must leave

In the midst of ecstasy is where we'll always be

"Lost In Gratitude"
7-24-19

Even in critical conditions, I find myself
Lost in gratitude
Appreciating my internal riches my peace of mind
And humble attitude
Expressing love and peace in the midst of hatred
And deceit
Utilizing my endurance not settling for temporary
Defeat
Thanking God for it all every lesson of the way
Staying mindful for every level of success there's
A price I must pay
Through trials and tribulations and months of having
Patience
I find myself lost in gratitude and suffering from
Appreciation
Had to learn from my lessons, things that wasn't
Taught in school
And still had to find my blessings while lost in
Gratitude

"Music Is Life"
1-1-20

Music can lift you up

When life brings you down

Music can be your company

When no one is around

Music can lift your burden

At times the world seems heavy

When life is out of harmony

Music can bring steady

With a shortage of places to go

Music can make you feel you belong

There's tons of inspiration

That can spring from just one song

Bringing healing to the sick

And adding purpose to your existence

Music will change your life

All while freeing your spirit

"Rich Beyond Measures"
1-3-20

Rich beyond measures with the love from above
Liberated from bondage growing wings of a dove
Knowledge that's gained is endless
Adding more to the gifts that are given

Rich beyond measures with the wisdom gained from trail
Now able to reach millions without having to go miles
The most precious gifts are priceless
Adding energy and spirit to the lifeless

Rich beyond measures with peace that grew from inside
Doing away with egos and killing diseases of pride
For every one gain, be prepared to give two
Because wealth is attained from what life gives you

Rich beyond measures with family and friends
Who are there through thick and thin good or bad till the end
So always keep them close and treat them as a prize
Because with "real" valuable treasures no price can be applied

"Seasons"

7-17-19

Your aroma is what caught my interest

You pick your colors to match your mood

It's like you have four personalities

And whichever one you choose is cool

I love the way you adopt change

And control actions of the universe

It's like its pain when it rains

When you hurt I hurt

I used to wonder if you loved me

Or did you even care

I know it's coming; the more you change

The better I prepare

But lately you've been having mood swings

So I don't know what to expect

Or should I take it as a sign

Of you letting me know what's to come next.

- 4 Seasons

"The Holy River"
12-24-19

Water that flows from the river to the bank

Has been purified and cleansed enough for us to drink

The river is refined and the water has been filtered

Only a fool would decline a drink from the river

Sensations roam the bottom and opportunity floats the surface

In between the two great miracles are working

The river is for renewing, drinking and bathing

If you're lost find the river it was created for saving

Purpose is being formed from the constant flow of water

The constant flowing river has gotten many things in order

Peace found in the river is enough to be shared

Arrive at the river broken, you're sure to leave repaired.

"Why Be Bitter"

8-13-2019

Why be bitter

When you can show affection?

Why be bitter

Instead of seeing the Lesson?

Why be bitter

Because it didn't go as planned?

Why be bitter

If you did the best you can?

Why be bitter

And show malice to someone else?

Remember bitterness is curable

But you must start with self....

ACTIVATE YOURSELF

"The Attitude That Grew From Relaxation"

11-13-19

Did you hear about the attitude that grew from relaxation

Proving history wrong learning to accept without having patience

With no pressure from stress it learned to address

Problems by being more relaxed

Congratulations to the attitude that grew from relaxing

And never went back to its past

"Where Do I Stand"
11-13-19

Where do I stand in life?

Is a question I sometimes ask myself

Searching for balance while using my talents

And still extending my help

Taken for granted while trying to manage

My problems and everyone else's

Never complaining but is it just me

Or does everyone seem so selfish?

To be understood by many and respected by all

Are things I constantly yearn

While the truth is often misunderstood

And respect is something you earn

With peace in my mind and love in my heart

I'm destined to conquer my plan

But still at times, I find myself

Wondering where do I stand

"Despising Lament"
11-14-19

To gain access to the peak

We all stand a chance

Greatness was installed at birth

The rest is in our hands

Be motivated by your dreams

Despite what others say or think

Success is the chain of life; if you struggle

Search for missing links

Strive to reach your peak

Without settling for less than the best

You only get one chance at life as we know

So live it with no regrets

"Bulletproof"

11-14-19

I hold your words close

And keep your advice near my ears

So whenever evil approach

It's your voice I seem to hear

Do not be afraid

No weapon formed shall prosper

In a world of rage

You're my protection as well as my doctor

Thanks for my Armor

I can now stand against the wiles of the devil

For it is not against flesh and blood

But against principles and powers I wrestle

Through lies and misconceptions

I struggle to find the truth

Never will I stop searching

I just pray I remain Bulletproof

So with my helmet, my shield and my sword

Please protect my mind and my heart my Lord

"Philanthropy"

11-15-19

Help a baby

Help a child

Help a lady

Help a man

As long as everyone helps one

We all have a chance

"Despising My Old Ways"

11-15-19

Arguing with recidivism

Going back and forth with relapse

At times, I am stubborn

And it becomes hard for me to see that

Some things can be reasoned

If I took the time to reason

But coquettish ways with my past

Puts a strain on receiving

So I'm done with the arguing

And no more going back and forth

Now I shall receive what's mine
For whatever that is worth

Vacenta

"Let Go and Go"
11-17-19

How far can I go

If I never look back

Just focused on now

And not on my past

How far will I go

With no judges of my choices

No hindrance from below

Only motivational voices

How far have I gotten

Since I've changed my way of thought

Though I don't look back on the past

I can't forget the route

"The Man Molded From Mud"

11-22-19

Battles and strains was all he knew

Grieving and pain became all but few

Wrongly accused oppressed and abused

His life became nothing but struggle

His time was spent and his mind was used

To find out the reason he suffered

With answers he found moved around

To alter conditions he faced

Once he started to usurp and learned how it work

His troubles begin to abate

Without giving up he's risen above

And conquered the trials of life

This the man who is molded from mud

With his mind and temple now ripe

"Over a Hill and Under a Bridge"
11-24-19

Over the hill and under a bridge
A badge of honor was presented
Out in the field and under the sun
A man of God was replenished

Over the hill and under a bridge
Is where a man stayed for days
The hill changed his mind
While the bridge changed his ways

Over the hill and under a bridge
Is where he will continue to pay homage
On top of the hill from under a bridge
His blessings now come in abundance

"The Rock That Cried"

12-1-19

Solid inside out but still possesses feelings
Purged on the outside but still needs cleaning
Pure on the inside but still needs healing
As things come to the light, eyes will be seeing
The rock once happy is the rock now grieving
But for every pound lost is only an oz that's receiving
Never lost faith and still continues to stride
So please don't judge the rock that once cried
While dying his tears and riding his pride
He now ready to smile with a head held high

"Intentional Kindness"

12-5-19

Extending a hand to someone in need of help

Can be a blessing for them and relief upon yourself

Look for something to give even if it's only a smile

What you say may go far but how they feel will go miles

Use kindness as a tool and also as a key

To help you get through doors and hold you at elite

The seeds that are sowed will bear nourished fruit

Kindness that is practiced is a good investment too

For some it's hard work but some it's facile

For some it comes speedy and for some it takes a while

"Ruthless Trust"

12-10-19

Brutally dependent

Faith is totally reliant

On the trust I place above

And the grounds of our alliance

The distance I've come

I've been carried along the way

Understanding as long as I trust God

I will always be okay

With all my trust in you

I'm able to move mountains

And understand if I can't,

I can always go around it

"Value"

12-9-19

Let your value speak for you

No words should have to be spoken

To prove to the world

You're the one who is chosen

To carry out your purpose

With a full fire and desire

Love and value what you do

And you'll never have to retire

"Today Is the Tomorrow"

12-11-19

Today is the tomorrow
All task must be finished
All jobs must be complete
And all goals must be achieved

Today is the tomorrow
All bodies are replenished
All stress is relieved
And all blessings are received

Today is the tomorrow
Mistakes are unknown
Doubt has been terminated
And strength has been shown

Today is the tomorrow
Love is displayed
Knowledge is spread
And heroes are made

"The Charming Tunnel Towards Light"

12-13-19

May the ones who wish to be free

Follow the path of light

Can't save the world

But the saving of one is enough to be right

The more you wish, the more you get

But that's only if you deserve

Every attempt is a charm

It's not only the third

The first is a lesson and the second is to strengthen

The third is referred to as a charm

Because normally it's just the beginning

Follow the path of the light

And respect the directions of wind

Because most great things start

When good things come to an end

"The Leaning Tower"
1-9-20

Standing very tall

But you can see it's slightly slanted

Years of serving the community

Much respect has been granted

Being honored became normal

Great remarks engraved with stone

But the question amongst many was,

What was it built on?

Weathered many storms

Of many different forms

But now it's starting to weaken

And hope is slowly decreasing

How long will this building stand

Against powers of inclination?

All that shall endure

Relies on strength of the foundation

Build on brick

And not on sand

Rely on God

And not on man

"Seize The Time"
1-10-20

While learning from your past and planning your future

Take the time to seize the moment

Let nothing stop you from gaining the necessary knowledge

You'll need to prolong it

Resources are contributors to levels of success

How about expanding yours?

Wisdom is the key for any address,

Which will unlock all doors

Take advantage of the moment at hand, but also,

Prepare for the moment to come

Utilize your experiences, knowledge and resources

Without forgetting where you came from

"Crumbs That Made the Loaf"

12-5-19

Piece by piece united in peace

The struggle overcame and birth a relief

Piece by piece united and free

Got rid of the I and adopted the we

Piece by piece united at least

We will continue to build and always increase

Piece by piece we will forever breed growth

And slice by slice we will create a loaf

"Excuse Excuses"

11-16-19

They're useless; they're stupid

So sit aside excuses

Don't make them; don't use them

They all bear fruitless

Don't decide on or choose them

Their allies are illusions

Excuse excuses

I know, yeah whatever

Excuses are irrelevant

So excuse them forever

"Finally Perfect"
12-6-19

Sometimes, things are done repeatedly

To learn how they're done right

When perfection does arrive

It's never over night

I've only loved once

But on many different levels

To find love is to search love

It don't always last forever

I'm finally finding my niche

After many years of searching

Grateful for the setbacks

And things that felt deserting

Sometimes things are done repeatedly

To learn how they're done right

We're not perfect but things can be perfect

As long as we keeping it tight

"Appreciate Your Weight...Wait"

8-30-19

As I look in the mirror

I feel like I need to gain weight

I eat a lot every day

But I'm still in the same place

Maybe I can't see, this is where I'm supposed to be

Until I accomplish what it is God has planned for me

As I look in the mirror

I feel sloppy and out of shape

I eat right every day

But still can't lose weight

Maybe I should stop grousing

And appreciate the extras

But keep working hard for my body to become better

No matter fat or skinny

Appreciate your body while you're in it

And realize God may have something for you

At the current size you're going through

"Searching For 20/20"

9-7-19

Look at the world through my eyes

And let me know if you see what I see

It may be difficult to envision

Some things despite how simple they may be

'Cause at times the smallest things can be the hardest to notice

So at times when you feel it's lucid truly tighten your focus

Use everything you notice to guide you from mistakes

And sometimes to see clearly, closing your eyes is the way

"Eyes in Time"

12-7-19

Greatness can happen fast but more often it takes time
A slow nickel can equal more than a quicker dime
Take small bites, so that everything is tasted
Cause at times with big bites, much flavor is wasted

Bio

Vacenta was born in a small town in South Carolina named Laurens. He was raised in a single mother household with two older brothers. His mother is one of the strongest Black Queens to walk the face of the earth. She made many sacrifices for him and his brothers and never complained or broke a sweat doing so,which is where he and his brothers adopted their ultimate grind from. Growing up he had a great love for sports, which he still holds close to his heart today. He was an All-Star in baseball traveling many cities and states to participate in different tournaments. During high school, he played football and ran track until he was expelled from school in the 11th grade. He later went to an alternative school where he received his GED which led him to college. He attended Gupton Jones College of Funeral Services in Decatur Georgia.

Atlanta is where Vacenta lived for three very long and fun years, in which the time his Son Kaden entered the world. While he attended college he would buy shades, belts, and Mac makeup and take it back to South Carolina and sell, which landed him the nickname "Mac Man". Following graduation, he landed a job at the funeral home where he did clinicals, Tara Garden Chapel. Later Vacenta was forced to move back to South Carolina where he reinvented himself and took steps back to move forward. This is the time he created the brand Kalfmuscle Gang, which is individuals who face adversities and overcome them with gratitude. Kalfmuscle is spelled with a "K" to signify the strength of being different.

Not long after that he found himself incarcerated in California where he spent two years and was inspired to write and pursue poetry. Upon his release, Vacenta has expanded his brand and mentored to different youth groups in his area. His goal is to inform and remind young adults that society cannot place limitations on them, to also use their mind as a tool to lead and guide them throughout the maze. The sooner you learn that the God in you is much more powerful than any other force, the easier it will be to notice, become, and act upon your purpose.

Vacenta would love for each of his readers to gain access to a broader perspective, tangible love, and a higher level of self-confidence, all which can help you reach the next level of your journey. There will be at least one tangible poem for YOU, keep it with you.